Achieve in 5!
Transform your life in just five minutes a day

by
Lesa Hammond, PhD

Library of Congress Control Number: 2012923946

ISBN-13: 978-0615673486
ISBN-10: 0615673481

Achieve in 5!
Transform your life in five minutes a day
New Way Press
www.newwaypress.com

Walnut Creek, CA 94597

THE BIGGEST ADVENTURE YOU CAN TAKE
IS TO LIVE THE LIFE OF YOUR DREAMS.
- OPRAH WINFREY

DON'T JUDGE EACH DAY BY THE
HARVEST YOU REAP, BUT BY THE SEEDS
YOU PLANT. - ROBERT LOUIS STEVENSON

TABLE OF CONTENTS

THE MOST EFFECTIVE WAY TO DO IT, IS
TO DO IT.—AMELIA EARHART

INTRODUCTION

*I*f you have goals that you have yet to make a reality, your life is about to change. You may have been drawn to this book because you have something you want to accomplish or because you are just curious what it means to *"Achieve in 5!"* This book will systematically help you realize every goal you truly desire. Whether it is a milestone to living a dream or crossing the finish line on a project you already started, *Achieve in 5!* offers a clear and easy-to-follow path for achieving your life's wishes.

For well over a decade, I have worked with people who want to change their lives. Most everyone's complaints fit within one of four categories: (1) unhappy in their career, (2) disappointed in their accomplishments, (3) goal-driven but unfocused, or (4) struggling with an unfulfilled dream. Most likely it is some combination of the four. It became my mission to help people change their lives. Experience has shown me that many people live what Henry David Thoreau called, "lives of quiet desperation." Years ago, I realized it was my mission to understand, and then facilitate transformation for those who have chosen to pursue a more fulfilling life.

Many of the people I have worked with have a long list of things they want to accomplish or things they wish they had achieved. The one thing I constantly hear is, "but I don't have time."

Several years ago, I began asking, "What if you spent only five minutes a day working to accomplish your goal? Do you have five minutes?" After some nervous laughter and suspicious looks, once they realized I was serious they all admitted that they could probably carve out five minutes a day to work on their goal.

Those two simple questions, "What if you only spent five minutes a day working to accomplish your goal?" and "Do you have five minutes?" led me to a personal experiment. For a month, I committed only five minutes a day to work on a goal. At the time, I was attempting to market a training program for women who were in career change. Marketing was not my strong suit and even though I was the one who suggested that five minutes a day would be productive, secretly I had my doubts. Could five minutes a day really bring me closer to achieving my goal? Would I actually commit to work on my goal five minutes every day?

One month later, I could honestly answer a resounding, "Yes!" The five-minute a day plan worked. At the end of a month, I had four new contracts in the works. That was more progress than I had made in the prior six months.

We all know that there are a lot of self-help books out there and all of them promise phenomenal results. So, why *Achieve in 5!*?

Achieve in 5! is a no-nonsense, practical, and simple way to get started working on those things that you think about but never get around to doing. Most of us with an unfulfilled goal spend hours a day thinking about what we should be doing.

If you are reading this book, I am sure you have at least one goal that you want to complete. Through the *Achieve in 5!* techniques you can accomplish it. With *Achieve in 5!* you will learn how you can make more progress in five minutes than you might typically make in fifteen or twenty. Whatever your desire – whether you want to start a business, begin an exercise routine, learn to play an instrument, market your products, network and develop new friendships, write a book, get rid of clutter…the list is endless–*Achieve in 5!* gives you the tools, techniques, and process to succeed.

Five minutes may not seem like much and of course, it is not. Do the math! If for the next year, all you do is work only five minutes a day on the goal you put off last year, next year at this time you will be thirty hours closer to reaching that goal. Thirty hours with a complex project is probably not going to get you close to finishing it, and *Achieve in 5!* does not say you can *only* work five minutes a day on your goal. What *Achieve in 5!* does, is have you commit to work on your goal just for that five minutes. After that, you have completed your commitment.

With *Achieve in 5!* you also learn how to turn five minutes of work into fifteen or more minutes of productivity. One technique is to keep your project in mind even when you are doing other things.

I used this technique in my role as a corporate trainer. At the end of a group activity, just prior to releasing the participants for lunch, I explained that when they returned, they would present their findings. When the participants returned, I gave them five minutes to prepare before reporting. When pre-warned, participants reconvened after lunch and they were ready to start the exercise and pull it together quickly. If I neglected to give those instructions before lunch, the participants had all but forgotten about the exercise by the time they returned. I had to allow a minimum of fifteen minutes for them to prepare before presenting. They had to take time to regroup and recall the exercise they had just completed before lunch. Groups that knew they would be presenting were able to enjoy their lunch and at the same time get prepared, both consciously and subconsciously. Invariably, the pre-warned groups made the better presentations.

You will take daily action for just five minutes. But, your goal will be a part of your *entire* day both consciously and subconsciously. So, when you sit down for five focused minutes, you will make more progress than you can imagine!

Are you ready to get started achieving your dreams by committing to work on them for only five minutes a day?

LET'S GET STARTED!

WHAT IS ACHIEVE IN 5!?

*A*chieve in 5! is easy to follow. Simply put, you identify what you want to accomplish, how you plan to accomplish it, and make a commitment to work on it for five minutes a day, every day. That's right-just commitment to work on your goal **five minutes** a day, **every day**.

When followed, *Achieve in 5!* is an infallible strategy, tool, and process for accomplishing your goals and achieving your dreams. With a minor commitment to work five focused minutes a day on your project, whatever it is, you will see amazing and surprisingly **quick** results.

THE POWER OF *ACHIEVE IN 5!*

"The less effort, the faster and more powerful you will be." –Bruce Lee

I know, and I'm sure you do too, that we find time to do the things that are most important to us. I also know that sometimes it is hard to put yourself first or to get motivated to do those things you say are important to you. Although you may think your goals are important, when they are competing with children, a career, aging parents, and relationships, your personal goals may take a back seat.

Achieve in 5! is a no-excuses program to move you forward towards whatever it is you want to achieve, whether it is cleaning a closet or building a business.

The power behind *Achieve in 5!* is that it takes the person with a dream, but no time or little motivation, to start moving forward on his or her goals and dreams a little each day. Over weeks or months, the five minutes will begin to expand as you take daily action and start to see results. The five-minute ritual becomes a habit and the habit builds momentum.

I wear earrings every day. If I forget my earrings one day, I feel quite under-dressed. I just do not feel complete. As you develop your *Achieve in 5!* habit, you will feel the same way if you venture to bed without engaging at least five minutes focused on your *Achieve in 5!* project.

I wrote this book using the *Achieve in 5!* method and while the book was constantly on my mind, there were some days when at midnight that I still had not written anything. When this happened, I would force myself to sit down at the computer and write for at least five minutes. On a few occasions, I was so tired that I could not keep my eyes open for even five minutes, so it was not focused time. I could not force myself to write. On those occasions, I would go to bed feeling a bit defeated. Without fail, two hours later, I was jolted out of my sleep by my thoughts. "*Achieve in 5!*" I would hear the voice in my head, "Get up now and do those five minutes." When that happened, I got up and not only did I do the five minutes; but when I went back to bed ten or fifteen minutes later, I was able to fall into a sound sleep. One interesting thing happened during those times. Often my writing during those ten minutes was some of the clearest conceptual writing I had done.

Achieve in 5! is a powerful tool. It turns achievement into a practice, a ritual, and a habit.

WHAT MAKES *ACHIEVE IN 5!* DIFFERENT?

There are many self-help products being sold. Self-help books, DVD's, and seminars can be found everywhere. Most of them say pretty much the same thing. They tell you that you can have anything your heart desires by following them. I have read several hundred self-help books focused on achievement. I have listened to countless audio programs, watched numerous video programs, and gone to dozens of seminars.

More than a decade ago, I found my mission. It involved devoting my life to finding a formula that would help people achieve their dreams. This formula had to work for the less-than-motivated as well as the highly-motivated achiever. *Achieve in 5!* is just that formula. My years of research led me to the discovery that many people do not achieve their desires, not because they don't know how or they lack ideas but primarily because they don't take those ideas to the finish line. They "give it the old college try" and quit. They put a burst of energy into a project then lose motivation or interest and move on to the next project. They hit a roadblock and stop dead in their tracks. Some of them even complete one milestone and mistake that for the finish line, or mistake the finish line for the dream.

When I stumbled upon the idea for *Achieve in 5!* I had started many projects and taken them to a point, and quit. With *Achieve in 5!* I learned follow-through. It is an easy way to keep moving forward until you reach the real finish line. Not only did it work for me, it worked for many others, and it was time to share it.

Will *Achieve in 5!* work for everyone? Yes, it will work for anyone willing to commit and follow through five minutes a day.

I have nothing negative to say about any of the self-help material currently on the market. I believe it all works, for some people. I know, for myself, that there are programs that have worked for me when I was clearly focused, followed them closely, and stayed consistent. However, many of them take so much time that my job and my life made it impractical for me to stay on course.

Some of the programs appear to be written for the single person who has lost her or his job or has another means of support. For the person who is desperate and highly motivated to change her life circumstance immediately, a high-powered program that requires four or five hours a day may be the best solution. *Achieve in 5!*, however, is great for the person who is comfortable but has a dream of something different.

Let me illustrate the difference between *Achieve in 5!* and many of the other motivational programs out there.

Even if you have never had a weight problem, everyone knows someone who has struggled with his or her weight. Let's talk about an anonymous friend for a minute. I will call her Sally. Sally is a close friend of yours and tells you her innermost thoughts. Sally needs to lose about forty pounds and she is impatient but not desperate. She knows it took her three years to gain the additional forty pounds she is carrying around, but she is eager to get rid of it and afraid that if she doesn't do it quickly she will lose momentum and not follow through with the program. So, instead of modifying her eating habits for life, possibly losing one to two pounds a week over a year, Sally decides to go on the very restrictive "Showgirl Crash Diet." She heard she could lose ten pounds a week on the diet. In four weeks she will be done.

Sally is very excited about the diet and is preparing to start. She read the book and watched the video about the Showgirl Crash Diet. Sally will eat nothing but rice cakes and two tablespoons of peanut butter each day for the first week. The first few days she tells you how great she feels. Day three, she starts to complain that she is really hungry, but she got on the scale and had lost two pounds, so it is worth it. Day four, she adds an orange to her meal. Day five, Sally starts looking at other diets that might work better and she tells you that she now hates rice cakes. Day six, Sally says she's lost eight pounds but will die if she has to eat another rice cake. You and Sally go to lunch and she has a salad. Half way through her salad, she reaches over and eats one, then two, then a handful of french fries from your plate. In less than a week, Sally has gained back the few pounds she lost and is back to square one. She is discouraged and disappointed with herself.

You may wonder, what does this have to do with *Achieve in 5!*? Well, *Achieve in 5!* is the slow and steady path that allows you to develop new habits and build and maintain momentum. Through small, daily actions, you reprogram your brain to achieve your desired results. *Achieve in 5!* also helps you to keep your mind on the ultimate goal, visualize the end result, and remain on course and steadfast regardless of other competing priorities. It is not the crash diet for achievement, telling you to get supercharged and excited about achieving your goal. It is the long-term life change that shows you how to set and achieve a goal over time. If you have a temporary setback, it is the process to help you jump right back on track.

THE KAIZEN CONNECTION

"The journey of a thousand miles begins with a single step." —Lao Tsu

Kaizen is the Japanese word for improvement. The word Kai means "change." The word Zen means "good." The philosophy of Kaizen is to make incremental improvements that are manageable so you will stick with them.

According to the Kaizen Institute, "Long-term success requires daily improvements." A first step in Kaizen is to create a list of things that need improvement. You start with the simplest and then move to the more difficult or more involved things.

Kaizen is a frequently trending topic on twitter and other social media sites. It became popular in America in the 1980s after its success in Japan. The Japanese used it as a way of creating superior quality products. Since that time, Kaizen has been applied to manufacturing processes, business processes, and more recently to personal life improvements.

You can combine *Achieve in 5!* with Kaizen as a life changing practice to improve areas of your life, eliminate bad habits and develop new ones.

KAIZEN EXERCISE

Begin by creating a list of things you want to change or improve in your life. Organize the list from the easiest and simplest to the most time consuming and most involved. Start *Achieve in 5!* with item number one, the easiest thing to change, then move through your list as each is accomplished.

TIME EXPANDS

Achieve in 5! is not a short-term solution to a long-term problem. If you have something you have wanted to achieve for a while, and it has not happened, seeking a short-term solution and instant gratification is probably not going to get you very far. If it does happen to get you moving, you may fizzle out as quickly as you got started.

Five minutes may not seem like a long time to work on achieving your dreams, and, of course, it's not long enough if you think you will reach the finish line in five minutes. You may think that you have to work long and hard to get things done. This is not true. There are many examples in everyday life where going faster and working harder does not equate to going further.

Think of the sprinter verses the long distance runner. Each type of runner has his place in the sport; but if the goal is to go the long distance, the slower runner with the steady pace will go much farther. Remember the story of the tortoise and the hare? The slow and steady tortoise beat the swift and overly-confident hare in the race.

Achieve in 5! is the tortoise approach. If you have a ten-page report to complete in two days, *Achieve in 5!* is not the correct tool. For that, you need something that is going to get you going at a rabbit's pace. However, if you have been avoiding going for your dream because you don't have the time, or the energy, or because life gets in the way, then you need something that is sustainable verses a rapid fire, quick-fizzle plan that has you working feverishly for a week and then abandoning your plans for the next year.

If you think that *Achieve in 5!* will take too long or that it is not enough effort, you are falling into the short-term thinking syndrome and a masochistic mentality regarding achievement. Generally, when sustained and permanent changes take place, they require consistent progressive action over a period of weeks, months, even years.

The goal of *Achieve in 5!* is sustained action. By committing five minutes a day to an action you will build momentum and eventually see yourself getting closer and closer to your goal. The whole concept of *Achieve in 5!* is taking very small and consistent steps toward your goal. If you can commit to work on your project for only five minutes a day, every day, you will find that you have made an amazing amount of progress in much less time than you anticipated.

Yes, five minutes is the commitment. Some days, maybe even many days, you will work more than five minutes as you see yourself making progress toward your milestone. However, the key to success is that you **only commit** to work for five minutes. When you have completed five minutes of work, you have completed your obligation. If you don't do another thing all day, you have done a great job and you can celebrate your success. That is *Achieve in 5!*

In this book, you will learn to navigate each step and identify your finish line. You will learn how to break your finish line down into manageable focused milestones. You will be able to identify and avoid the things that are holding you back from success.

HOW *ACHIEVE IN 5!* WORKS

When I started *Achieve in 5!* as an experiment, it was one that I primarily developed for myself. I do not consider myself a super-high-achiever or a driven individual, but I do have things I want to accomplish. As much as I thought I wanted to accomplish them, I found myself thinking, "I don't have the time to make this happen."

I am a bit of an idea machine. I come up with idea after idea. I have thought of many ideas for new books, innovative products, and creative services. So many, in fact, that it would be hard to put a number to them. From time to time, I would even start to work on one of them, but at some point in the process I would lose focus. I would let the idea sit stagnant for so long that I completely forgot it or lost interest in it. At other times, I let other people's lack of enthusiasm for my idea affect my energy and desire to work on it. There were even times when I was simply too afraid to take that next big step to make it happen. Whatever the reason I stopped working to manifest my idea, the result was the same. The idea never came to fruition; or maybe worse yet, it came to fruition as someone else's idea. It wasn't that someone stole my idea; it was an idea that's time had come and somebody (other than me) knew how to bring it to life.

My experience is not unique. Many people have ideas and do get them started. I share this pattern because maybe you are where I have been. Although there are certainly those people who were totally focused at nineteen and those who found their passion, knew how to pursue a dream, and have never questioned any aspect of their life. They are the exception.

There are also people who were totally focused at nineteen and now at thirty-five, or forty, or sixty, realize that they were not following their own dream at nineteen and now they are ready to discover and follow their true passion.

I have personally experienced both. I know how things worked when I was motivated, driven and committed to accomplishing my goal, as well as how they did not work when I was not. When I found my life mission of helping people achieve their goals and unlearn scarcity thinking, I went back to school to understand the process and theory of transformation.

When I was working on my dissertation, I was totally driven. My pursuit of a doctoral degree was not to have three additional initials after my name. It was to gain specific knowledge so that I could live my life mission. My dissertation was an expression of and a route to pursuing my passion. Nothing was going to stop me from accomplishing my goal.

Even when times were tough and things went wrong, I knew I would complete the dissertation. In fact, I had a personal goal to complete my dissertation within a year after completing my coursework. When I got negative feedback on my research, I adjusted and kept pushing forward. I was on a mission. After one not so positive meeting with my advisor, I did spend three days in bed without talking to anyone; but that was only a temporary and very short-lived setback. I was determined to succeed, and therefore I did.

I had a very clear picture of what it would be, what it would look like, and the doors it would open for me as a result of my research. I was focused, I was 100% committed to accomplishing that goal. I worked at it consistently and conscientiously for five years.

Obviously, you will not get a PhD if you only work on it five minutes a day. However, by committing to work five minutes a day, I remained on course and I gained momentum during the journey.

THE PROCESS

Achieve in 5! is a five step process. Following these five steps will prepare you to achieve any goal you set and to live your dream:

1. **Visualize** what you want (the dream), where you want to be (the finish line), and major steps you need to take to get there (the milestones).
2. **Crystallize** your dream and mark your finish line. (How will you know that you have finished the race?)
3. **Chart** your course and mark your milestones.

26

4. **Identify** the first *Achieve in 5!* milestone and commit to work on it five minutes a day every single day until you reach it.
5. **Refine and repeat** until you pass each milestone and cross the finish line.

This small book offers a full explanation and carefully walks you through each step. In it, you will find the basic explanation of *Achieve in 5!* and begin the process toward living your dream.

As you start on this journey, let me familiarize you with the distinction between three terms: dream, milestone and finish line. Although the three words are similar, they have different functions and represent different levels of progress.

The "dream" is a future reality you envision beyond the "finish line." The finish line is a designated endpoint of the journey. "Milestones" are key accomplishments along the way to the finish line. I will also use the word goal and project from time to time. "Goal" is used in context to refer to actions related to the finish line, a milestone, or a distinct and concrete step on your journey. I will the terms "step" or "landmark" to refer to smaller but significant activities on route to reaching the milestone.

THE DREAM

My college friend Richard is an example of a person who had a dream. He knew the finish line. He marked his milestones and identified his course along the way. From the time Richard walked into his first class at Ohio State, he knew that he wanted to be a college professor. The class that brought his dream into view was a basic Psychology 101 class that fulfilled a general education requirement. The class was in a huge lecture hall with over 300 seats and a student occupying every seat. It was the kind of classroom setting that intimidates the average freshman. Instead of being intimidated, Richard fell in love with the class, the lecture hall, the subject, and the idea of being the professor standing in the front of the room with wide-eyed freshmen staring at him as he enlightened them about the inner workings of the mind.

After class, when most of us were talking about where we would go dancing on Friday night, Richard was talking about the psychologist Piaget and his theory of cognitive development. Richard loved the idea of spending his days expanding the minds of young college students. He could see himself in front of the large lecture hall, writing on the board and engaging 300 students as he talked about "the way the brain synthesizes data." When Richard was finished with his coursework of the day, he would read books and articles on psychology, neuroscience, and epistemology (the philosophy of knowledge) as his form of entertainment. Richard had a passion and he had a **dream**.

THE FINISH LINE

For Richard to live his dream he knew he would need to get a PhD and get teaching experience. Richard mapped out a course of action. He planned *backwards* from his first teaching job at a large well-respected university. In Richard's case, finishing the degree and securing a faculty position in a large university was his finish line. Only after he reached the finish line would he really be able to live his dream.

THE MILESTONE

For Richard, there were many <u>milestones</u> before he could live his dream:

- ✓ complete his general education requirements
- ✓ make sure each of his professors know him and like him
- ✓ get involved in a research project with one of his professors
- ✓ become a teaching assistant in his junior year
- ✓ get his bachelor's degree with a high GPA
- ✓ get accepted into a university that offered a PhD directly from a bachelors
- ✓ get a job as a research assistant during graduate school, and impress his professors so that he would receive excellent recommendations
- ✓ secure a faculty position

Going back to his first goal, in order for Richard to complete his general education requirements with good grades he needed to study for each assignment. The on-time completion of each assignment with a grade of "A" is an example of a "step" or "landmark" on the way to reaching his milestone.

FIVE STEPS TO *ACHIEVE IN 5!*

*T*his section will walk you through the five-step process of setting your goals. The amount of time you spend working through this session will depend on the complexity of your *Achieve in 5!* project.

Again, the steps are:
1. **Visualize** what you want (the dream), where you want to be (the finish line), and major steps you need to take to get there (the milestones).
2. **Crystallize** your dream and mark your finish line. (How will you know that you have finished the race?)
3. **Chart** your course and mark your milestones.

4. **Identify** the first *Achieve in 5!* milestone and commit to work on it five minutes a day every single day until you reach it.
5. **Refine and repeat** until you pass each milestone and cross the finish line.

If you are planning to clean a closet, you may breeze through the exercises in this section. However, if your dream is life changing, you may need to spend more time carefully reading and thinking through the exercises in this section.

VISUALIZE WHAT YOU WANT

The first step to *Achieve in 5!* is to know what you want. If you do *not* have a clear idea of where you are going the chances that you will reach a desirable destination diminish greatly. As the famous baseball player and coach Yogi Berra said, "If you don't know where you are going, you might not get there." It is important to have a clear picture of what you want to achieve. Whether your desire is to clean a closet, write a book, or start a business the steps are the same. You must first have a clear vision of your outcome.

Picture what is beyond the finish line. When visualizing your dream, it is important to get in touch with your motivation for this outcome. The size of your dream does not matter. Whether you dream of having a clean and organized closet or you dream of being the next Oprah with your own television network and a household name, the process is the same. You must be clear about why the dream is important to you. What will life be like when you are living your dream?

WARM-UP EXERCISE

In the space below or in a separate journal, respond to each question:
- What is your dream?

- What is the last step, the finish line, before you can live your dream?

Once you determine your finish line, visualize it. Involve all five senses and ask yourself:

- What does it look like?

- What does it feel like?

- What does it sound like?

- What does it taste like?

- What does it smell like?

- How will you feel having reached this finish line?

Now, mentally step over the finish line and fast forward six months:

- What has the past six months of living your dream been like?

- Spend some time each day visualizing your dream. This should not take extra time during your day. You can do this right before you fall asleep, right after you wake up, in the shower, while cooking, exercising, or engaged in some other activity. Be as you were when you were a child. Daydream. Let yourself go to the future state where you are living your dream. At this stage, your visions of living your dream may shift and that is okay. When you follow the steps to crystalize your dream, that is when you will create a steady picture of where you are going.

CRYSTALLIZE YOUR DREAM AND MARK YOUR FINISH LINE

Think of this journey as a marathon. Once the marathon committee decides on the location for the race, they then determine the course and mark the finish line. Once that is completed, they do not change it. When you are running the race, no one is moving the finish line at the end of the track.

If you are planning to run a marathon, can you see yourself with your arms up, crossing the finish line and putting the medal over your head and around your neck? Your dream is what you visualize as the result of crossing the finish line. Crystallizing your dream is necessary to mark your finish line. The finish line is a concrete goal just before you live the dream.

Too often, people set their finish line far short of their dream. I have heard many people identify getting a degree, creating a website, or writing a book as their finish line, but their dream involves having an exciting job traveling or being a recognized expert in their field. None of the actions mentioned above will automatically make the person realize that dream. Although there may certainly be milestones along the route.

Dave Thomas, the founder of Wendy's Hamburgers, dropped out of school after the tenth grade and became a millionaire. Regretting that he never finished high school, at the age of 61 years, Thomas hired a tutor and took the high school equivalency examination. In Thomas' case, receiving his high school diploma was a finish line.

If what you have identified as your finish line is a means to an end, rather than an end itself, it is not a finish line. The finish line is the end just before living your dream.

Let's suppose that you are creating an online business: What is your dream related to that business? Maybe your dream is that you go to bed and wake up each morning to find over 100 orders of your product sold while you were sleeping. If that is your dream, then you determine the final action that will get you to that point. At a minimum, you will need a product, a website, customers, and a method for fulfilling orders, but what is the finish line? Once you have identified or developed your products and you have created your website, the hard work begins. Driving people to your website and getting them to purchase your products is the real work.

Many writers think that completing their book and getting it published is the finish line; however, unless you do not care if anyone buys the book, then having a published book is a milestone. It is certainly a big milestone, but nonetheless, it is a milestone on the way to your finish line. The finish line needs to be the final step of completion before you feel that you have fully succeeded with your project and before you are able to live your dream.

Another common mistake people make when visualizing their dream is to make it too picturesque and unrelated to what they want to achieve. When I asked one of my career transition workshop participants, I'll call her Shawna, to describe her dream, she closed her eyes. She began describing a very charming scene of relaxing on the promenade deck of a cruise ship and waving to a passing fleet.

Although it was a beautiful image and description, it had nothing to do with what she said she wanted to accomplish. What she described sounded more like a vacation. Shawna could easily have taken a cruise without having to accomplish anything except booking and paying for the trip. Shawna wanted to be a photographic journalist, or to get paid to travel and take pictures.

Had Shawna said that she could see herself on a fully paid cruise to Africa taking pictures of passengers on the promenade deck, that would have been a clearer dream. She might have said she could visualize her photographs in a travel guide advertising a trip to Africa. Now, with those dreams Shawna could decide on her finish line.

When Shawna first decided her dream, she did not even own a good camera. She had a small automatic camera that took decent pictures, but nothing close to professional photography. Shawna was in her late forties at the time. Her children were grown and she was ready for a career change. She wanted to travel and she loved to take photos. Determining the finish line in Shawna's case was a bit of a process since she had no idea of what it would take to be a traveling photographer. But, after some work, Shawna decided that her finish line would be to get her first paid job as a photographer with all expenses paid, and it had to be a job outside of the country.

Once you have a picture of your dream clearly planted in your mind, it is important to crystalize it. In this step, you clarify what is driving your desire to reach the finish line.

There are several ways of crystalizing your dream. Pick the one that works best for you or do all of them:

- **Visually Create Your Dream** – If you are artistic draw, paint, collage, or sculpt your dream. Create a picture that represents what you will be doing on the other side of the finish line. Maybe you want to sculpt yourself speaking in front of large audiences, or create a collage of all the people who are doing what you want to do just beyond the finish line.

- **Write a Narrative** – If you are a writer, write a story in present tense of your life or a typical day just beyond the finish line. The story should have complete detail. If you are a poet, write a poem or a song that creates a picture of your dream for you. Craft that dream into a realistic story of your life, your daily activity just beyond the finish line. This is not a tale of fantasy or your life twenty years from now when you are making millions of dollars through passive income. This is not your obituary (as some programs have you do). This is the point just beyond the finish line.

- **Record Your Dream** – If you are a storyteller, get a tape recorder and turn it on. First, with your eyes closed describe in detail living your dream just beyond your finish line. If you choose this option, do it four or five times. Create a great story that you can play again and again. Play it when you are driving, sleeping, and doing chores.

- **Carry a Token** – One interesting way to crystallize your dream is to carry a token of something that will always remind you of your dream. It could be a rock, a charm, or some other token that is a constant reminder of where you want to be. One woman I know purchased a charm bracelet and put all of her milestones on the bracelet and took them off as each milestone was reached. The final charm represented her dream. Her goal was to have an empty charm bracelet and put the final charm on a necklace she would wear. She planned to gift the charm bracelet to someone struggling to achieve a dream.

As you are crystallizing your dream, you may want to think about the answers to the following questions:

- Why do I want this?

- What will it mean to me to live this dream?

- What activities will I engage in each day when I am living this dream?

- Who will be involved in my life and how will these people be involved as I positively live my dream?

- How will I describe what I do for a living?

Create your personal dream reminder. Using one of the exercises above or something else, Crystalizing your dream is a personal process. You can be as creative as you want. You just want to make sure that whatever you do, it is something that will constantly remind you of your dream. Refer to the exercise above and create your reminder.

CHART YOUR COURSE AND MARK YOUR MILESTONES

Charting your course involves listing all of the milestones that will get you to your finish line.

If you want to write a best-selling novel, and make a living from your writing, you may list the following actions:

- Write my first novel
- Get an agent and publishing contract
- Sell one million copies of my books

Those three milestones are significant. Now, look at what it takes to achieve each. Depending on what your book is about you may need to research your subject. If you do not have a reliable computer, you may need to buy a computer or go to the library and use one. If you have not already done so, you may want to read or reread other books in the same genre.

List all of the things that go along with getting to the finish line. Brainstorm, but be realistic, and do not include minute details. For example, if you need to do research on the subject, you do not have to list the types of research or where you will go to get the information. Simply list *Research*. You want to write the list and keep it for reference, but you do not want to spend too much time on the list. If you are spending five minutes a week on the list, you are allowing it to distract you from working on your *Achieve in 5!* task.

Your list might look something like this:

- Write my novel (milestone)
  - Write the book
  - Research key information
  - Edit (many times)
- Get an agent and publishing contract. (milestone)
  - Subscribe to WritersMarket.com (goal)
  - Write query letter (goal)
  - Send letter to 10 agents (at a time)
- Sell first 100,000 copies (milestone)
  - Get publicity (goal)
    - Create a website (goal)
    - Create a blog (goal)
    - Write articles (goal)
    - Get my professional photo taken (goal)
    - Contact television and radio programs (goal)
    - Join speakers bureau (goal)
    - Get speaking engagements (goal)
- Make a living from the royalties on my books (finish line)

This list is certainly not exhaustive. And, as you can see by this example, you have a lot to do!

It is a good idea to get a journal, a notebook, or use your computer to keep information related to your current *Achieve in 5!* project. Refer to it frequently. The most important milestone as you get started is the first. However, you will want to revisit your list often and possibly revise it as you complete one milestone and begin the next. If you keep your dream and the finish line at the forefront of your mind as you *Achieve in 5!*, you can achieve it.

WARM-UP EXERCISE

Create your list of goals and milestones.

TAKING A MORE CIRCUITOUS ROUTE

When I first started down this path toward living my dream, the picture of what I wanted was quite out of focus, to say the least. I could see multiple finish lines. I could not figure out the milestones, but there were some landmarks that I could identify.

I would head toward a milestone and half-way there I might identify my next milestone. I knew I wanted to make a difference in the world. I knew I wanted to impact the lives of others, but I had no idea what that would look like or how I would do it. My plan was equivalent to knowing that I wanted to go overseas, but with no particular destination in mind. As far as my finish line went, it could be Europe, Asia, Africa, or Antarctica for that matter.

Because of my lack of clarity on a finish line, I had many false starts. I reached some milestones only to realize they were probably taking me in a direction I did not want to go. On other occasions, I would start toward a milestone and midway realize I needed to change course.

This rather circuitous but eventful route did eventually help me to clarify my finish line. Truthfully, I don't know if I could have clarified it without my many false starts. So, if you are having difficulty clarifying your finish line, start toward a milestone and examine your motives. Pick a goal and take action now. Continue to visualize your dream until you can crystalize it.

Keep in mind there is more than one way to get involved in running a marathon. Some people, like my husband, set a goal to run a marathon even though they are not runners. My husband joined a marathon preparation team and prepared for six months. He systematically built up to the twenty-six mile run. He walked and ran the twenty-six miles and completed the race. That was his goal. It was his first and probably his last marathon, but he began with a clear finish line in mind.

Other people start out running for their health or for fun. They start with a block, slowly build up to a mile, five miles, ten miles and eventually decide to run a marathon. Running a marathon may not have been the original goal, but over time, with multiple successive milestones, a new goal is set and a new finish line emerges in their mind.

Running a marathon might seem like an odd metaphor for *Achieve in 5!* since you could not run a full marathon in five minutes. However, you can develop the habit of running by starting with five minutes a day. You can run twenty-six miles by running five minutes a day.

Achieve in 5! involves taking five minutes of concentrated action per day with no distractions during those five minutes. If you start with five minutes of running even very slowly and then increase your speed and distance a bit each day you will soon find yourself running a half mile in five minutes. Then maybe one day, you will decide you want to run a full marathon.

SELECT ONE *ACHIEVE IN 5!* GOAL

Selecting your first *Achieve in 5!* goal is where the magic of the process is revealed. It is not just picking something on your list and working on it for five minutes a day. You will want your *Achieve in 5!* goal to refer directly back to your first milestone.

Achieve in 5! is about taking direct action. For the new runner, researching running shoes is not an *Achieve in 5!* activity. Running for five minutes is an *Achieve in 5!* activity. So, commit to taking **direct** action toward your first milestone, five minutes a day every day.

The process of selecting your *Achieve in 5!* goal requires knowing yourself. The objective is not to let your strength become a detriment, but to build on your strengths and continue to work productively on your goal. If you tend to get caught up in research and never start a project, or never finish it because you are researching too much, then you want your first *Achieve in 5!* goal to be an action.

If your *Achieve in 5!* milestone is to **write a book,** then for five minutes a day, write. You can do research, you can start your website, but until you have the book finished, you will write five minutes a day regardless of whatever else there is to do or what other activity you decide is also part of your dream.

Selecting an *Achieve in 5!* goal can be challenging for some people. The *Achieve in 5!* goal must be something that is concrete. The key is that it must directly move you toward your finish line. It must be an action step. Many people create activity around their goal, while never taking direct action to achieve their goal.

Here is the clincher. You will get your best results if you make your *Achieve in 5!* goal the part of the milestone that you most resist. That's what I said; **make your *Achieve in 5!* goal (action) the part of the milestone you most resist.**

If you want to start a consulting business, making business cards, getting letterhead, developing a website, and reading books about consulting all sound like good goals related to different milestones toward starting your business. However, they are probably not the activities that will help you get your practice off the ground. The only thing that will get your practice off the ground is to bring clients into your practice.

I can hear you now. You are saying, "But I need business cards." Yes, you do. However, you probably are not resisting getting business cards. You are resisting bringing in clients. Your *Achieve in 5!* goal must be an action that will get you the result you want. As I said before, you will get the best results if your *Achieve in 5!* goal is the thing you most resist doing.

WARM-UP EXERCISE

What is the action you most resist related to attaining your dream?

Committing to work on your action five minutes a day every day is a discipline you master through practice. The aim is to make your five minute a day commitment an essential habit. Like brushing your teeth, taking a shower, or eating breakfast, *Achieve in 5!* should be a habit. As you begin, work directly toward your first milestone every single day, including weekends. If you miss a day, jump right back in and keep working at it. Like any discipline or practice, you are not expected to be perfect, but strive toward excellence.

REFINE AND REPEAT UNTIL YOU CROSS THE FINISH LINE

Once you have completed your initial *Achieve in 5!* goal, start back at step number one and relive your dream (reliving your dream should be a daily practice), revisit your finish line, refine your milestone, and set a new *Achieve in 5!* goal. Reach your first milestone before you move to a goal in another milestone. Remember *Achieve in 5!* is a sequential process that moves you from landmark to milestone to finish line to living your dream.

YOUR ACHIEVEMENT ARCHETYPE

I have identified six achievement archetypes. Each archetype has unique characteristics in working toward goal attainment. *Achieve in 5!* can provide a helpful framework for each archetype. Keep in mind that your achievement archetype might shift as life circumstances change. *Achieve in 5!* is used differently depending upon which archetype is most prominent for you at the moment. You may even see yourself in multiple archetypes; and you may have different archetypes depending on the project at hand.

No archetype is preferable to the other. They are simply different and can use the *Achieve in 5!* process slightly differently. By identifying your achievement archetype you will see how *Achieve in 5!* can best work for you.

THE SLEEPER

The Sleeper has dreams but has trouble turning them into action.

The Sleeper archetype has great ideas, and wonderful dreams, but cannot seem to make them happen. Sleepers seem stuck dreaming. Onlookers may wonder if they are ever going to get off their duff and start the process of making those dreams come true. Sometimes it appears Sleepers do nothing but dream. From the outside it is hard to know what is really happening. It may appear someone is a Sleeper when he is really percolating and forming a clear plan for progressing forward. Once awakened, this type of person may become a goal oriented Sprinter or Marathoner.

I remember a young man, Earl, who was a classic Sleeper. Earl talked about flipping property. He loved to watch television shows like *This Old House*, *Flip This House* and every other home improvement show on television. After all, Earl had 452 channels controlled by the remote that appeared glued to his left hand, as he lay comfortably on his couch in his undershirt and boxers. Earl may have been preparing mentally and physically to launch his home

54

flipping business, but to the onlooker Earl was a Sleeper disguised as a Couch Potato.

If you relate to the Sleeper archetype, you are probably feeling stuck. You have dreams and know it is time to act on them. Complete the exercise below to begin acting on your dreams.

SLEEPER WARM-UP EXERCISE

As a Sleeper, you will benefit most from *Achieve in 5!* by taking five minutes now to write your favorite idea, follow the *Achieve in 5!* process and start moving. Tomorrow, begin *Achieve in 5!* with one concrete action.

THE PREPARER

Preparers are in a holding pattern when they get stuck in the preparation stage.

Preparers want to have everything set before getting started. Preparers buy all the equipment they need to get started. They sign all the preliminary paperwork. They have every material thing they could possibly need to get started towards their goal.

The problem with the Preparer is, by the time she has all of the tools she needs, she has lost the drive to go for the gold. Preparers have to realize they are in a holding pattern when they get stuck in the preparation stage. Preparers are generally afraid of starting, so they use the preparation as a way to delude themselves into thinking they are taking action. The preparer can do this regardless of whether it is a business, an exercise program, writing a book, or some other project.

You are a Preparer if you can personally relate to Sherry's story. Sherry was planning to start her own business. On the surface, she had it all together and was moving at a steady pace to get her business up and running. She had business cards, a registered business name, letterhead, and a logo. She then developed a website and was in the process of incorporating, but the business never got beyond the concept phase.

Before starting an exercise program, the Preparer must buy new exercise clothes, the latest equipment, books, magazines, and a gym membership. By the time all of those things are purchased the desire to exercise has long passed.

Preparers can benefit from *Achieve in 5!* by taking the first step to actually get going:

What are you resisting the most?

What would be the first direct action to truly get your project off the ground?

Do it! Stop preparing. Take a step toward real action. At this moment, forget about preparing, don't write anything. For the next five minutes make actual progress toward your first milestone.

THE SPRINTER

Sprinters can pace themselves to finish the long race.

The Sprinter is the person who gets a flurry of energy around a goal and is up nights working on it. The Sprinter accomplishes an amazing amount in a very short period of time. The problem for the Sprinter is that in most cases when it comes to achieving his dreams, the Sprinter doesn't realize he is in a long distance race. It takes more than two, three or even six months to achieve most big things. If you are a Sprinter, you have probably started a lot of projects, you may have even finished the project itself, but you don't make it to the other side of the finish line.

Are you an artist with a lot of almost finished paintings, a writer with almost finished books, a scrap-booker with almost finished scrapbooks? Do you run out of steam in the middle of a project? If you are a Sprinter, there is hope. The good news is that you have energy. You can get moving on a project. The bad news is you lose momentum because you don't know how to pace yourself. The good news is that you can learn to pace yourself.

Achieve in 5! is perfect for helping the Sprinter cross the finish line. Because the Sprinter's energy serves him well in the beginning it is best for the Sprinter to reengage with a dropped project and use *Achieve in 5!* to take the project to the finish line.

SPRINTER WARM-UP EXERCISES

Decide which project you want to complete. Begin working on that project for only five minutes each day. Once the momentum kicks in, you will want to work on it hours at a time. Go ahead. Then when you run out of steam, take a short break (no longer than a week). After your break, start working only five minutes a day every day. This pattern works best and almost exclusively for the Sprinter.

THE ANALYZER

No amount of analysis will prevent failure. You fail if you don't start.

Analyzers spend their time researching how to do everything. They want to know the whole process before they start. They seek advice from anyone who will give it and may go off on wild goose chases trying to account for every detail and every scenario. Analyzers forestall achievement by laying the groundwork until the idea fizzles or they get so much negative input that all they can see are obstacles. Analyzers are similar to Preparers in that they are really afraid to make the big move.

By researching they think they are avoiding the possibility of failure. In truth, they are avoiding the possibility of success, because they never start. You have probably heard the phrase "analysis paralysis." That is what happens because analyzing anything enough will make it seem overwhelming.

Analyzer, you cannot avoid the possibility of failure. You fail if you don't start. Logically, you know that, and you have possibly even researched why you cannot seem to move forward on your goals.

ANALYZER WARM-UP EXERCISES

The Analyzer, like the Preparer, needs to take the plunge. Follow the five steps to *Achieve in 5!* and begin. There is no amount of research that will guarantee your success.

THE JOGGER

Joggers have a passion for the activity. They would love nothing more than to devote full time to it.

Joggers start out with a slow steady pace, continue at that pace, and can seem to go forever. At one level, this is the constant state that *Achieve in 5!* is designed to help you reach and sustain. However, the Jogger archetype can have one drawback. Some Joggers have no destination. They are doing what they do for the sheer pleasure of the experience. They love the feeling that comes with the activity itself.

The Jogger may be the guy who works 9:00 am – 5:00 pm in a bank and comes home every evening and begins refinishing furniture. He refinishes furniture for his family, his friends, and anyone who will lend him a table. This is absolutely wonderful, as long as he is happy doing this. However, unless the Jogger secretly has a dream of doing nothing but refinishing furniture, he is probably unfulfilled.

You may be a Jogger if you have a hobby that you do in your free time and you secretly dream that you could turn this hobby into your livelihood. Maybe you don't know how to make it your livelihood or you are a bit afraid to try.

As a Jogger, it may be as if you are on a treadmill with your passion. One participant used *Achieve in 5!* to turn her secret passion for jewelry making into an income source. She had over a hundred pieces of jewelry that she had made, sitting in a drawer. It was time for her to get off the jewelry making treadmill and to start taking action to monetize her passion.

JOGGER WARM-UP EXERCISES

If you are a Jogger, you can use *Achieve in 5!* to help chart the course for turning your hobby into your livelihood, so that you can live your dream. Use the five-step process to turn your avocation into your vocation.

THE MARATHONER

Marathoners always cross the finish line, but at what cost?

Marathoners are self-motivated and will keep running as fast as they can (with direction) and purpose until they cross the finish line. They are deliberate and methodical before their next big run. Marathoners are on task and on track with their goals. Their vision is clear, they know where they want to go and they move steadily toward it. To anyone looking on, the Marathoner is successful and possibly a bit of a workaholic.

Achieve in 5! may appear to be the least useful to the Marathoner if they are on goal and living their dream. However, Marathoners sometimes are so focused on one area of their life that they miss out on the other areas. They may be exceedingly successful in business, but neglect their family and friends.

For anyone of any archetype to be totally fulfilled, it is important to live a well-rounded life. Marathoners may use *Achieve in 5!* to slow their pace in the area they consider the marathon, and chart a new, fulfilling course for the other areas of their life.

You, the Marathoner, can take a look at your whole life. Are there parts of your life that you have neglected?

If so, what is the mental picture you have for your total life? Describe it.

Chart your course for one of those neglected areas and use *Achieve in 5!* to get on track with living your dream.

THE PRINCIPLES

*S*ome simple principles will keep you on track with *Achieve in 5!*. As you go about your day, keep these principles in mind. Write them on an index card, make a note on your computer, or set reminders on your smartphone. Look at them frequently and keep moving forward, five minutes at a time.

THE PRINCIPLES
➤ I TAKE CONSISTENT PROGRESSIVE ACTION
➤ I CAN QUIT
➤ I KEEP *ACHIEVE IN 5!* ON MY MIND
➤ I SEE THE FINISH LINE
➤ I ANNOUNCE MY COMMITMENT
➤ I PERSEVERE UNTIL I CROSS THE FINISH LINE

I TAKE CONSISTENT PROGRESSIVE ACTION

The concept of consistent progressive action might be the number one success factor for *Achieve in 5!*. By working on your goal for five minutes a day, every day, you create a pattern of action and keep the project firmly planted in your mind. By doing this, your *Achieve in 5!* project becomes an omnipresent force that you subconsciously strategize and process.

Consistent progressive action makes your five minutes extremely productive and brings you closer and closer to living the dream at the end of the finish line. By taking daily action, you will find that you want to spend more and more time working on your *Achieve in 5!* project. Just remember, five minutes is all you need in order to have achieved your daily goal.

I CAN QUIT (BUT I WON'T)

I used to think that it was important to not make quitting an option, but that just didn't work. I found that I quit more things when I thought quitting was not optional than when I realized I had free will and could quit anytime. Quitting is always an option. Committing to something with no option to quit can be

66

daunting. Most people have probably quit more things than they have finished. So, you know, you can quit. The choice is yours. The real question is, "Are you going to quit?"

When we know that we have options, alternatives, and freewill it becomes easier to make the right choice. If we choose to quit, we know it is a choice and not someone else's fault. We made the decision consciously and hopefully for good reasons.

Now you can say, "Of course I can quit; but I won't."

I KEEP *ACHIEVE IN 5!* ON MY MIND

With *Achieve in 5!* you commit to working five minutes a day toward your goal every day. One of the key benefits of this process is that the consistent daily action keeps your goal omnipresent in your mind. By knowing that you must take concentrated action for at least five minutes a day, you will think of things that remind you of the actions you will take. You will think of things that help move your goal forward. Your actions will reflect your thoughts as they relate to your goal. By making your daily action a part of your routine, it will seep into your thoughts throughout the day.

Write your current goal and carry it with you everywhere you go. Make it readily visible, so that you read somewhere, anywhere, at least five times a day.

I SEE THE FINISH LINE

Seeing your finish line is an essential element to your success. Seeing is the act of visualizing what it will really be like. The ability to visualize your dream and the finish line, is part of making your dream a reality. It is important to get a clear picture in your mind of the end result, how it looks, what it feels like, and how you feel emotionally having completed it.

As a part of *Achieve in 5!* make it a daily ritual to practice, multiple times a day, seeing (visualizing) yourself crossing the finish line.

I ANNOUNCE MY COMMITMENT

This is a bit controversial. Some experts will tell you to keep your goals private until they are either completed or near completion. While there is a certain level of wisdom and safety in this secrecy, I suggest announcing your commitment to your dream, your finish line, or your goal once you are resolved to achieve it.

Some of the greatest clarity I received regarding *Achieve in 5!* happened as a result of talking with people who were interested in following the plan but were supportively skeptical. They asked good questions and discussed how it would fit with their particular situation. Making your announcement can be frightening and can open you to negative input from others. If you feel you are going to get a negative response or less than supportive feedback from someone, don't talk about your plan to that person.

When I made my announcement about *Achieve in 5!* one of my colleagues simply replied, "What is it you are up to now?" Although I am sure the statement was not meant to be discouraging, it didn't sit well with me. I changed the subject and never again engaged the topic of *Achieve in 5!* with her. While making your announcement is a great motivator, make sure that you are committed to achieving your goal before you make the announcement. Make the announcement to a supportive and honest group. Do not tell people who will give insincere support or who will be negative.

If you are not ready to make the announcement to your family and close friends, create or find a support group.

I PERSEVERE UNTIL I CROSS THE FINISH LINE

This is the big commitment. Making the commitment to persevere until you cross the finish line means you will succeed. You will not just try. You will not give up. You will not fail. **You will succeed** or, literally, you will die in the process of trying.

Have you heard the story of Cliff Young? I first heard of him on a video titled, _Seeing Red Cars_ by Laura Goodrich. The story of Cliff Young is as follows:

> _Cliff Young was an Australian sheepherder. Every year, there is a 544-mile race from Sydney to Melbourne. It is considered the world's longest and toughest ultra-marathon. The race takes approximately seven days to complete. Big sports companies like Nike and Adidas sponsor the athletes. Most of the athletes are younger than thirty years old and are_

equipped with the most expensive training outfits and shoes. Cliff Young was a sixty-one year old farmer who entered the race. He showed up for the race in overalls and galoshes over his work boots.

When the marathon started, the professional runners left Cliff behind. Instead of running, he appeared to be shuffling his feet. Some onlookers laughed. There were also the compassionate viewers who watched the live broadcast of the event and prayed that someone would stop the crazy old man before he collapsed and died.

The professional athletes knew it took about seven days to finish the race. They would run eighteen hours and sleep six. Cliff Young had not trained for the race and he did not know the rules. He just liked to run. Cliff did not stop running at the end of the first day. Although he was still far behind the world-class athletes, he kept on running. He ran and waved to spectators who watched the event from the side of the highways. He didn't stop to sleep at night.

Cliff Young won the race. He ran the 544 miles in 5 days, 15 hours and 4 minutes. That was *nine hours ahead of the second place winner. Now, when running the Sydney to Melbourne race, almost nobody sleeps. To win that race, they have to run like Cliff Young did, they run around the clock until they cross the finish line.*

Perseverance is often more important than skill or knowledge. If you are to succeed you must make a commitment to yourself that you will persevere until you cross the finish line.

SUCCEED WITH *ACHIEVE IN 5!*

*I*f you truly want to achieve a goal and if you have any free time at all, you have five minutes. If you cannot commit to five minutes a day to achieve your goal, what is holding you back? I have identified some common barriers to achievement. They are:

- Old baggage
- A lack of focus
- Other people's needs
- Your comfort zone
- Perfectionism
- Other people's doubts
- Procrastination
- Inertia

You may suffer from more than one of these barriers at any given time. The key is learning to overcome them.

IS OLD BAGGAGE HOLDING YOU BACK?

A few years ago, I attended a presentation where the speaker did an interesting demonstration. He had a cardboard box with the front cut out so that the audience could see what was inside. He had a hole cut in the top of the box. The hole was just big enough for a small hand to fit through. He asked a boy of about six-years-old to come on stage. The speaker had the child put his hand through the hole in the top of the box. He then handed the boy a colorful toy through the open front panel of the box. The toy was too big to be pulled through the hole.

The speaker said the toy cost about ten dollars, and everyone could see that it would obviously be fun for the boy. He said the child could keep the toy if he was still holding it after the speaker finished counting to "five." The speaker then walked about ten feet away from the boy and said he had a $50 gift certificate from Toys R Us. With the gift certificate the child could buy whatever he wanted at Toys R Us, but if the boy wanted the gift certificate he had to let go of the toy.

Puzzled and still grasping the toy, the young boy said, "I don't understand." The speaker explained the rules again and described what the child could possibly get with the gift certificate. He also explained that in order to get the gift certificate the child would have to let go of the fun toy that was already in his hand.

The child stood for a minute looking puzzled and then said, "Oh, I get it."

The speaker then began his count, "ONE..."

The child dropped the toy and ran to the gift certificate as fast as he could. By the count of "TWO" the certificate was in his hand.

What are you holding onto, that if you let it go would free you to reach your goal and get to the finish line faster? What beliefs, what things, what people are acting as an anchor to your progress? Are you holding tight to those things that look good—or maybe just look familiar—but are keeping you from making the progress you need to make?

IS A LACK OF FOCUS HOLDING YOU BACK?

One of the most common concerns I hear from people is that they have many ideas but cannot focus on one long enough to complete it. They start a project and end up changing course in a different direction before completing it.

Many people have great ideas. As I mentioned, I have many great ideas myself. Until I realized that it is impossible to keep all of the ideas in my head and work on them at the same time, I was unable to complete any of them. A Chinese proverb states, "The man who chases two rabbits catches none."

If you are an idea person, pick one idea. Make a commitment to take that idea to the finish line before you start on the next one.

Achieve in 5! is perfect for helping you focus on one idea at a time. As the syndicated cartoonist, Ashleigh Brilliant said, "Good ideas are common–what's uncommon are people who'll work hard enough to bring them about."

ARE OTHER PEOPLE'S NEEDS HOLDING YOU BACK?

Do you put other people's needs before your own? If you have small children, of course you put their needs before your own. Maybe you put the needs of your job before your own needs, or you put the needs of your spouse or partner before your own needs.

If you are a caretaker, in reality or just in personality, you probably find it difficult to make time for yourself. If you can't find time for yourself, you will never find time to bring your dreams to fruition.

We all have obligations and by no means am I suggesting that you neglect them. Your obligations are important and following through on commitments is important. Yet you may be able to do much more for others if you are able to accomplish the things that are important to you.

Achieve in 5! works well for the person who has many responsibilities. It is for the person who takes care of others, be it a child, parent, spouse, or some other loved one.

If you spend only five minutes each day focused on your goals you will make personal progress and feel proud that you are taking care of yourself as well as others.

Though it might be ideal, most of us cannot afford to spend hours each day working on our personal life-transforming goals. With *Achieve in 5!* you can create a plan that will work for you and with your obligations.

IS YOUR COMFORT ZONE HOLDING YOU BACK?

"If you put yourself in a position where you have to stretch outside your comfort zone, then you are forced to expand your consciousness." —Les Brown

Understanding your comfort zone can help you get off to a good start with *Achieve in 5!* Each of us has our own comfort zone. Your comfort zone is what feels familiar. Whether good or bad, it is familiar and you know what to expect.

The interesting thing about the comfort zone is that we don't even have to be happy in it or want to stay in it. Because we have become used to things a certain way, when things change or we are exposed to something different it makes us uncomfortable.

People often stay in bad situations because they are within their comfort zone. We may not like the situation, but at least it is familiar and we know what to expect. We stay in jobs where we are miserable, stay in relationships that are abusive, continue poor eating habits, and do not take the next step to make our lives better—all because change is uncomfortable. An English idiom, "Better the devil you know than the devil you don't," supports staying in your comfort zone and not branching out for a potentially better situation.

Our comfort zone is a powerful, important, and unique aspect of each of our identities. The comfort zone is a defense mechanism that warns us when a situation may not be safe. The problem with that is that our comfort zone does not know the difference between unsafe and unfamiliar. Sometimes situations that are familiar are far more unsafe than situations that are unfamiliar and outside of our comfort zone.

Do not allow your comfort zone to be the determining factor of how far you will go and what changes you will or will not make. If you follow the guidance of your comfort zone, you are giving an irrational emotion the power to define your limits, define who you are, and who you will remain.

I am not saying ignore your comfort zone completely, it is important to acknowledge feelings of fear. They may be genuine indicators of danger. If you are walking down a street at night and feel nervous and think, "I should stay on the major streets because I don't know the neighborhood," go with that feeling. It might be an indicator of an unsafe area. However, if you are supposed to make a speech that could help your career and you feel nervous about making that speech and think, "I might look really stupid if I make this speech" that is an indicator that you probably need to practice the speech more. If you know that making the speech is going to help you get ahead, practice, practice, practice, and force yourself out of your comfort zone.

Your comfort zone can shift and expand. The more experiences you have, the more people you interact with, the more you read, the more changes you make, the broader your comfort zone will grow. The broader your comfort zone, the more you can achieve.

To change your comfort zone, you must first step outside of it and risk feeling uncomfortable. There are four phases to changing your comfort zone. Once you recognize the need for a change and begin to make that change, you can track the natural reactions attached to the process.

Phase I – Ready
Phase II – Reluctant
Phase III – Willing
Phase IV – Able

PHASE I - READY

In the beginning, Phase I, you recognize a need for change. You might think, "I'm Ready! I can do this." You may be eager to get started. In Phase I, you may even know that it is going to be uncomfortable and a bit of a stretch for you, but you still think, "I can do this."

In truth, you have no idea of what is really required to make the change. Only after getting started, only after gaining some knowledge and beginning the process, does it become apparent just how much harder this is going to be than you originally thought. Doubt and insecurity begin to set in, and you have moved to Phase II.

PHASE II - RELUCTANT

Phase II is where self-doubt comes in. It is the most dangerous phase to your success. This is the most common phase. Not only does it feel uncomfortable, you realize how hard it is. You may have setbacks that cause you to feel like you are not able to succeed or it is not worth the effort. You may simply be miserable and feel you made a mistake trying. This is the phase where you have stepped outside of your comfort zone. In Phase I, while you may feel a little discomfort, you are still within that comfortable realm. Phase II is the BIG step, the stretch, the "make it or break it" stage. If you keep working at it regardless of the discomfort, doubt and mistakes, you will turn that corner and move into Phase III.

PHASE III - WILLING

In Phase III, you accept that this is hard. You know you have stretched beyond your comfort zone, you know that with hard work, perseverance and endurance you can succeed. It is not easy to accept your shortcomings, but you know it is possible. You know that if you continue, you will eventually succeed and set a new comfort zone. There is still some danger of turning back, as in Phase II, because you know that you have turned a corner and a setback or a big mistake may again lead you to feel you should give up. If you stick with it, you will move to Phase IV.

PHASE IV - ABLE

When you have moved to Phase IV, you have expanded or shifted your comfort zone. Your new behavior, new job, or new experience is now second nature. You may remember that it was hard in the beginning, but now the memory is usually somewhat vague. Experiences that may have seemed devastating at the time are remembered as some of the best lessons of your life. In fact, once your comfort zone shifts, it becomes difficult to think of things being any other way than how they are right now, in your new comfort zone.

ARE YOUR THOUGHTS ABOUT SUCCESS HOLDING YOU BACK?

What goal are you trying to achieve? If you are hoping to launch a successful business, do you have negative thoughts about successful business people? If you have a dream of making a living as an artist, do you think that all artists are poor and are you afraid you will end up living in your car?

What do you fear about success?

I overheard a friend's daughter say, "Rich people are evil." Those statements whether made out of envy or seemingly made in jest, are statements that enter the psyche and can make it difficult to acquire any significant amount of money. For the person who is trying to lose weight, unspoken negative thoughts associated with thinness can sabotage any good diet. For the craftsperson who wants to make a living selling your craft, if you grew up thinking of crafts as a hobby not a profession, it may be holding you back. Some people have gained a significant amount of weight after having a traumatic event that they subconsciously associated with being thin or being attractive.

What sabotaging statements do you make to yourself about the state you want to achieve? Can you change that belief? Can you rephrase your statements?

It is the time to take control of your life, five minutes at a time.

WARM-UP EXERCISE

If you have negative thoughts about success, this exercise will help you shift your thinking.

Think of all the sabotaging statements you have heard, made or thought about the life that you want to live. (*For example:* Managing a business is too hard and too time consuming, entrepreneurs don't make time for their families.) Write those statements now.

On a separate piece of paper, change each statement into a positive phrase. (*For example:* People who manage their own business have the flexibility to live life on their own terms. Many people have a successful business and a fulfilling life.) Keep your positive statements with you and read them every day for a month.

IS PERFECTIONISM HOLDING YOU BACK?

As I look around and see the people I know, most of them are high achievers and have high expectations of themselves; but what does that really mean and how does it serve them?

In an email exchange with a friend, I was bemoaning that in one week I had three people tell me that they could not do *Achieve in 5!* All three actually told me that they did not have time for it.

Her response was profound. She said, "Isn't it crazy that five minutes is such a big deal? Part of it may be that they are 'perfectionists' and don't want to commit and fail to follow through. I feel badly when I'm not doing as well as I would expect of myself."

Many of us suffer from perfectionism and although it can be an admirable quality, it also sets us up for failure. There is almost no way that you can write the perfect book, have the perfect start to your business, have the perfect body, raise the perfect child, or cook the perfect meal. I could go on forever with the list.

Being perfect is an unrealistic expectation to place on ourselves. What is this desire to be perfect? What does it mean if you are less than perfect? Have you failed?

In a program I developed over a decade ago, I explained the Truth about Failure and Success. If you don't finish, have you failed? If you give something a try and it doesn't work out the first time, have you failed? If you complete it but it is not as good as you know it could be, have you failed?

If you suffer from the "If I can't do it right, I'm not going to do it at all" syndrome, you will miss many opportunities in life. Doing things right is a good thing, but doing the right thing takes stamina, insight, wisdom, and perseverance. Doing the right thing might mean it does not work perfectly the first time. It means, if you know where you are going and have an idea of how to get there, and if you persist until in the end, then you succeed.

I am sure you have heard that Thomas Edison tried thousands of ways to invent the light bulb before he got it to work. He never considered those attempts as failures. Forget about being perfect. Forget about failure. Pursue your dreams with confidence and know that you will succeed if you keep moving forward.

ARE OTHER PEOPLE'S DOUBTS HOLDING YOU BACK?

As I mentioned in a previous chapter, there are conflicting opinions about whether or not you should share your dreams and goals with others before you are securely on your way to achieving them. Some experts believe you should not share your goals because having others know that you are pursuing a dream is opening the door for all of their insecurities to be thrust upon you. Others believe that sharing your goals and dreams is a way to get help that you otherwise might not be aware exists. It also makes your commitment stronger because you have put it out there.

You may have shared an idea or dream with someone who immediately told you all of the reasons it would not work; moreover, you may have shared a dream with someone who didn't say anything but left you feeling judged.

There may be people who would be very happy to see you fall flat on your face. Your success may be a threat to their security and sense of comfort with you. Your success may also ignite their feelings of inadequacy. However, I have found that most dream-squashers are not typically out to ruin your life or sabotage your success; they truly think they are helping. These are good-hearted souls who just don't want you to get your hopes up and then not succeed. They are doing their best to be supportive.

There comes a point in your process when you know that you have to achieve your goals and all of the naysayers in the world will not stop you. At that point, you can confidently share your plans with anyone. Until then, choose your confidantes carefully and if you happen to confide in someone who, regardless of their intention, feels like a dream-squasher, brush yourself off and spend five minutes engrossed in your passion. See what you can *Achieve in 5!*.

IS PROCRASTINATION HOLDING YOU BACK?

The untold secret about procrastination is that it can be addictive. Yes, some people are actually addicted to procrastination.

There seem to be two types of students at opposite ends of a continuum. Student "A" is the one who is given an assignment of a term paper and plans her paper the first day the assignment is given. She takes steady and consistent daily action to produce the best term paper she can. Student "Z," on the other hand, receives the assignment of the term paper thinks about it a bit, forgets about it a bit, and knows he should be working on it, but he doesn't. Then two or three days before the rough draft is due he works feverishly, pulling all-nighters. Student "Z" receives accolades from the teacher for great work. You may notice similar patterns with some of your coworkers or fellow students.

If you are like Student "A" you may wonder how Student "Z" pulls off such feats. However, if you have the pattern of Student "Z" you probably feel a bit of envy toward Student "A." You wish you could motivate yourself to get started earlier with the same level of enthusiasm, focus, and inspiration you have when the clock is ticking.

It is no mystery why some people thrive with the deadline looming. The ticking clock produces multiple emotions. Real fear is sensed as you realize you are in jeopardy of missing the deadline. This is when both hormones and chemistry combine to produce the effect that allows you to stay up and focus all night. It even sparks a level of creativity that otherwise would not have occurred had you followed a more reasonable path to completing your goal.

Adrenaline is the hormone that is responsible when you hear those stories of a 100-pound woman lifting a car off her child. It is the "fight or flight" hormone that is released in times of fear. When adrenaline is released, the blood vessels and air passages dilate. This allows more blood into the muscles and more oxygen into the lungs, increasing physical performance for short bursts of time.

Endorphins are the chemicals released by the brain during times of stress and pain. They act as natural painkillers and can create a euphoric feeling. When you are working on a short deadline, you are under physical and emotional stress, and the body reacts by releasing adrenaline and endorphins. These natural drugs make you a happy, stimulated, productive and creative machine. No wonder some of us thrive on procrastination!

At this point, you may think I am advocating procrastination. Procrastination can be addictive, and like a fine wine, it can be beneficial when used correctly with the right combination of ingredients, but when abused can ruin lives.

In most cases, the detrimental results of procrastination far outweigh the benefits you get from it. You are probably aware of the negative impact it can have - costing you money, damaging relationships, and maybe worst of all, causing you to run out of time on your dream.

If you have a dream, if you are seeking to achieve something that is big to you, procrastinating to get started or procrastinating in the process is one sure-fire way to make it *not* happen. Making forward progress over a long distance takes consistent progressive action. You could not wait until three hours before you needed to be in a city 5000 miles away before you booked the flight or took off on the road. You also cannot expect to achieve a large long-term goal overnight or over the weekend.

If you have ever had to pay a late fee or if you thought of the perfect gift for a friend but waited too long to buy it and the store sold out, then you know the problem with procrastination. There is generally a price to pay when you procrastinate.

The key to all success is to clearly identify your finish line, identify your milestone, set goals to reach your milestone and work at it consistently. Commit to working on your goal five minutes a day—and keep at it. Making action a consistent practice will break the procrastination addiction. With commitment, consistency and practice, you will find yourself as creative in small increments as you are when the clock is ticking.

IS INERTIA HOLDING YOU BACK?

Isaac Newton developed three laws of motion. The first, relating to inertia, states that an object in motion tends to stay in motion and an object at rest tends to stay at rest until acted upon by an unbalanced force. The natural tendency of objects (or people) is to resist changes in their state of motion. This is inertia.

You could have been steadily working toward your goal, seldom missing a day, and then life happened. Maybe you went on a vacation that was such a diversion that you could barely remember what you were doing to achieve your goal. Maybe you had a very big project in your day job and although you met that deadline, your passion was put on hold and now you are finding yourself unable to get back in the swing of working on it. Possibly a short-term illness was the culprit. When you were sick you couldn't focus enough to work on your project, then when you got well, you just could not get back in the groove. Maybe some other event took you off track, but now you just cannot get restarted. Inertia has set in.

While writing this book, inertia set in for me. I cannot remember what took me off the *Achieve in 5!* path, but something did and even though I thought about writing every day, I could not energize myself to sit down and write. I felt guilty because I was not writing, but that did not move me to write. I watched a different movie almost every night. I read a few interesting books on motivation, marketing and other topics tangentially related to *Achieve in 5!*. I mentally beat myself up a bit and tried to give myself a strong kick in the butt, but not much worked—until I decided to take my own advice. I set a goal to write five minutes a day, every single day.

On day one, my writings were incoherent and ended up being discarded. On day two, I created this section and named it "Is a Lack of Motivation Holding You Back?" I wrote for five minutes. When I returned to the chapter on day three, I started writing and I realized it wasn't really a lack of motivation, it was an inability to get back on course. I was stuck. Inertia had set in.

The key was to disrupt the inertia. I had to impose an unbalanced force against the state of rest. I realized that *Achieve in 5!* was the answer to inertia. By doing *Achieve in 5!*, I recalibrated and regained my momentum. In the beginning, I resisted and I did it anyway. As you can see, it worked, or you would not be reading this book!

Almost everyone has lapses in their achievement process from time to time. Whether your setback is due to competing priorities, mild depression, short-term illness, or some emergency that took over your life, *Achieve in 5!* is the perfect remedy for getting back on track. The best way to return your state of enthusiasm and action is to do something, anything, directly related to your milestone for five minutes. That five minutes will eventually take hold and you will be back on course.

ON YOUR MARK...GET READY TO
ACHIEVE IN 5!

"One important key to success is self-confidence. An important key to self-confidence is preparation." — Arthur Ashe

*B*efore you begin *Achieve in 5!* spend one week preparing. Proper preparation is the best way to start any journey.

BE HONEST WITH YOURSELF

For you to get the maximum results out of *Achieve in 5!* all you have to do is commit to working on your goal five minutes a day, every day. That is really all you have to do. The only thing about that is, some people will not follow through and work on their goal five minutes a day every day. They will admit that *Achieve in 5!* "probably works." They say they want to achieve their goal. They admit that they can find five minutes a day. Still, they manage to let the day pass without completing even five minutes. Bill Cosby is quoted as saying, "You have to want it more than you fear it."

If you believe you have a goal that you want to achieve, but you are not willing to give it five minutes of your time every day, how much do you really want to achieve it? What are you gaining from not achieving it? What is stopping you from making the commitment? Think about this seriously. What is stopping you from working on your goal five minutes a day? Where is the source of your resistance? Confront the reason you resist acting on the thing that will help you to have a more fulfilling life.

I see that you have two choices. One is to get in touch with and deeply understand the underlying source of your resistance and work through that—which might take years of therapy. The other is to make the commitment to do *Achieve in 5!* regardless of the resistance and regardless of your comfort level. As the Nike motto says, "Just Do It."

COMMIT TO ONLY FIVE

I often hear people say, "*Achieve in 5!* is great, and I plan to spend longer working at my goal than five minutes a day." One ambitious soul said she might even spend two hours per day on her goal. Although these are ambitious ideas, there is a reason this program is called *Achieve in 5!*. That's because you are to commit to five minutes per day; not 10, 20 or 30 minutes, but five minutes.

If you start *Achieve in 5!* thinking you will spend thirty minutes, my guess is you have tried that strategy before—spending thirty minutes a day on some goal. It is also my guess that it didn't work. I presume that if you do jump in spending thirty minutes or an hour initially, you will be gung ho for the first day, three days, or maybe even the first week or two. Then there will come a day when you legitimately do not have time to spend an hour on your goal, so you will miss a day. That day will mark the beginning of a nice long hiatus. This is precisely why *Achieve in 5!* was developed.

Most people agree, five minutes is a manageable time commitment. Now I admit, you will not become a tennis pro in five minutes a day and it will take you quite a while to write the great American novel if you only write five minutes a day. If you commit to work only five minutes a day, in forty-five days you will be much closer to having the great American novel than if you wrote for one hour one day and didn't have time to get back to it for a month or two.

If you follow *Achieve in 5!* and commit to only five minutes a day, momentum will kick in and there will be many days when you work at your goal longer than five minutes; but you **must** make your commitment only five minutes a day. Making the commitment longer is the first formula for not following through with it.

MENTALLY PREPARE

Another component of *Achieve in 5!* is to remember to prepare for your five minutes. Mentally think about the time you will spend. When I started writing, I would only spend five minutes writing a blog. The blog was always on my mind. I knew I had to write for five minutes and I knew those five minutes had to be productive. I would get inspiration for the blog well before I sat down to write. When it was time to write, I knew the topic and had a mental outline of the flow. I may have even scribbled some key points on a piece of paper hours before. The blog time included anything I need to do to complete the blog. For example, in a blog in which I referred to Steven Covey's *Seven Habits of Highly Effective People*, I did a quick internet search to insure I included the right categories. That was included in my blog time, so don't think you have to spend hours preparing for your five minutes.

Preparation time is important, and depending on the preparation, you might want to include it in your five minutes, or you might want to make it separate. Keep in mind, *Achieve in 5!* time is about doing. Things that are directly related to achieving your current milestone are considered in your five minutes. Anything else, is not *Achieve in 5!*.

During the *Achieve in 5!* process, your only preparation will be time you spend engaged in activities that are unrelated to your *Achieve in 5!* goal. You will think about what you need to do for your *Achieve in 5!* time or maybe on your way to the store you will pick up stamps if you are planning to mail something during your *Achieve in 5!* time. If getting stamps is a part of your five minutes that day, that works too.

The key is effective, consistent, diligent action—five minutes at a time.

YOUR MOST PRODUCTIVE FIVE MINUTES

For me, it works best to allow my *Achieve in 5!* time to be fluid. I don't pick a certain time of day or a certain place to do my *Achieve in 5!*. If I wake up in the morning and have some extra time, I do my *Achieve in 5!* at that time and I know that I have met my commitment for the day. That doesn't mean that I won't return to work on my goal later that day, but if I do not get back to it, I feel satisfied that I have met my commitment. Other days, I get busy and by the end of the day I am completely exhausted. I know I have to complete my *Achieve in 5!*. Even if I am tired and ready to go to bed, possibly even too exhausted to think, I do my *Achieve in 5!*. When I wait until close to midnight after a long busy day, the quality of what I do is usually not as good as it would have been had I worked on my goal while I was awake and energized. However, even when I wait until five minutes before I pass-out from exhaustion, it is a great feeling to know that I spent five minutes and met my commitment to work consistently on my goal every day.

100

It does not help to have a goal and feel guilty that you are not accomplishing it. You can carve out five minutes a day. The real question is, are you ready to achieve your goal? Is the goal important to you? If the answer is yes, then commit only to five minutes a day and you will find that you are making more progress than you ever imagined possible.

THE EBB AND FLOW OF MOTIVATION AND ENERGY

Most of us are not constantly motivated and ready to tackle the world at every moment. We are not machines that have a steady pace and can continue at that pace for months, maybe years, on end. There are ebbs and flows to the motivation and energy we have. There are times when we might go weeks or months at a high speed, then the time comes when we need some downtime. If you become ill, stressed, or overworked in other aspects of your life, it can be difficult to maintain motivation for the things you ultimately want most.

The other most common time your flow moves to an ebb, is when you are butting up against your comfort zone. If you are making steady progress and then you hit an unproductive or uncreative wall, or you lose energy for the project, this can be a sign that you are about to make a major breakthrough. When you hit the edge of your comfort zone it is natural to get stalled. You are venturing into unchartered territory, or at least the territory is unchartered by you. Sometimes just putting one foot in front of the other is the best remedy for getting through those periods. One of my favorite lines from the movie *We Bought a Zoo* was, "All you need is twenty seconds of insane courage and I promise you something great will come of it."

At times like this, it is more important than ever to keep moving forward. Keep your five-minute commitment. If you are truly stuck, seek some supportive and intelligent outside advice. Do not ask friends and family who will support you in "resting" or quitting!

There are definitely times when it is important to rest and rejuvenate. However, relaxation and rejuvenation have a way of being both friend and foe. If you have a job and you are working for someone else—a job that is bringing home a regular paycheck every week, or two, or month—then you probably have vacation time as a part of your benefits package.

If you are like many people, you take a week or two of vacation once a year. And, if you are like most people, when you return from vacation after that week or two off, you are not ready to jump full-force back into your job. It takes a day or two to reconnect and readjust to working. If you had no deadlines or tasks awaiting you, it might take even longer to regain focus. You might start on something totally unrelated to what you were doing when you left for your brief vacation.

You will have days, maybe weeks, when you just don't have the same level of energy and motivation that you have when you are really in the flow of your project. You may not even feel like you want to put in five minutes. Maybe you had a busy week at your day job or you had a stressful week at home. During those times, it is more important than ever that you continue to move steadily toward your milestone with your commitment to work on it five minutes a day.

Even if what you do during those five minutes does not seem productive, the fact that you are continuing and working diligently toward your goal is what is important. That commitment will get you through your ebb and have you ready to move at great speed when your energy and motivation return, which they will.

Cutting back on constant action is not a bad thing. Everyone needs time to rest and rejuvenate. The problem comes when the goal that you were so consistently striving to achieve becomes less important after the rest. You may lose interest in that goal, or you get an "even better idea" while you are resting. If you have been consistently keeping your commitment of working on your goal five minutes and maybe you have worked more than five minutes many days, then stick with exactly five minutes when you are in the ebb. Do not stop, stall or change course. Keep moving forward, five minutes a day.

When I was consulting and had to prepare for a new workshop, I worked late into the night and got up very early in the morning for days in a row. By the fourth or fifth day, the only thing I want to do when I arrived at home was to relax. The last thing I want to do was to spend five minutes writing and thinking. This was exactly when *Achieve in 5!* was most important. Continuing to do JUST five minutes a day helped me maintain my focus. It kept my milestone present in my mind, and it helped me to keep moving forward.

If you allow yourself to get stalled by a temporary ebb in your motivation, that temporary ebb can result in total derailment. Do not let this happen. Spend five minutes a day on your goal, even when you have neither the energy nor the motivation. You will be thankful that you kept moving forward, because when the motivation returns you will be right on your charted course.

IF THE LADDER IS NOT LEANING AGAINST THE RIGHT WALL, EVERY STEP WE TAKE JUST GETS US TO THE WRONG PLACE FASTER.—STEPHEN R. COVEY

GET SET...

You've read about *Achieve in 5!* and you know that it is something you can do. So, you have made the decision that you are ready to begin. All you need to do now is prepare. It is best to prepare before you launch your five minute per day routine. It is hard to do everything you need to do to prepare by only committing five minutes. However, if you only have five minutes a day, then certainly start by using the five minutes to prepare. Do not let the need to prepare delay your ability to *Achieve in 5!*

START AN *ACHIEVE IN 5!* SUPPORT GROUP

One of the most effective ways to increase your motivation and commitment is to be a part of an *Achieve in 5!* support group. If you are interested in, and focused on achieving a goal, having a group of like-minded, positive and supportive people working with you is one of the best formulas for success.

If you can find one or two other people who are doing *Achieve in 5!*, meet with them regularly or check in by phone, text, or use some form of social media to keep in touch. Having both the online support group and your personal group is best.

The key to the support group is to keep each other on track and honest. Check to see whether everyone did their *Achieve in 5!* each day between your meetings. Ask about the progress each member made. Support each other. As long as a member did at least five minutes a day, their effort is to be congratulated and celebrated. This is about process as much as progress. *Achieve in 5!* is neither a race nor a contest. Think of it as a practice or a ritual of consistency.

Hold each other accountable. If a member of the group is staying within their comfort zone and not taking direct action to move close to their milestone, call them on it. Ask what help they need to get back on course.

The support group must be a positive, honest and helpful experience and because time is of the essence, keep your meetings short. Keep them positive. If possible, have a meeting that has a dual purpose. One support group decided to have *Achieve in 5!* walking meetings. The members take a walk and talk to each other about their progress at the same time.

A word of caution: Do not fall into a trap of spending more time in the support process than working on your *Achieve in 5!* goal. If you meet for two hours a week and each member is spending only five minutes a day on their goal, you will eventually find the group experience draining, or that you are using the group to put off moving your goal forward.

DEVELOP YOUR PLAN

Remember the five-step process for *Achieve in 5!*:

1. **Visualize** what you want (the dream), where you want to be (the finish line), and major steps you need to take to get there (the milestones).

2. **Crystallize** your dream and mark your finish line. (How will you know that you have finished the race?)

3. **Chart** your course and mark your milestones.

4. **Identify** the first *Achieve in 5!* milestone and commit to work on it five minutes a day every single day until you reach it.

5. **Refine and repeat** until you pass each milestone and cross the finish line.

Now it is time to take action and plan your *Achieve in 5!* journey. Get your journal, small notebook, tablet or computer and answer the following questions. Keep this journal with you or close to you at all times.

ACHIEVE IN 5! PLANNING

A. Write out what your dream day would look like. What is on the other side of the finish line? What goals do you want to achieve? Get in touch with your motivation for wanting to achieve these goals. Write the description of your perfect day after you have crossed the finish line.

B. What is the last thing you will need to do or have before you can live your dream? Write that in as much detail as possible.

C. What are three to five major milestones you will need to pass on your way to the finish line?

D. What is the first milestone? Write it out in detail.

E. What is the first step that will allow you to make major progress toward that milestone?

F. What is the thing you are most resisting that will move you toward the milestone? Write the activity that you most fear or that you are most resisting in clear terms, so that you will know when you have conquered it.

Congratulations, you are on your way to Achieve in 5!.

DISCIPLINE IS THE BRIDGE BETWEEN GOALS
AND ACCOMPLISHMENTS.—JIM ROHN

GO...THE FIRST 7 DAYS

*A*lthough *Achieve in 5!* is a practice and a life-changing strategy, it requires some work to make it a habit. For this reason, this section will guide you through the first seven days.

The first seven days of *Achieve in 5!* are critical. They set the stage for your future success or failure with your project. While *Achieve in 5!* is designed so that you commit to work on your project five minutes a day every day, remember some days you will work longer than five minutes. However, during the first seven days, it is essential that you work only five minutes a day.

I have seen people get excited about *Achieve in 5!*. They have a lot of energy those first few days. They want to work an hour or two or more on their goal right away. They then set the mental expectation that they must work at least

113

one or two hours to have been successful that day. This is the number one recipe for failure.

You will not work on the goal one hour or two every day. If you were likely to do that you probably would have done it already. It is important that you make it clear in your mind that five minutes of work is a successful completion toward your milestone. For this reason, **I strongly recommend that for the first week you only work five minutes a day on your project.** Whatever you do, do not work more than fifteen minutes a day on your *Achieve in 5!* project for the first week.

You are ready to start *Achieve in 5!*. I guarantee, if you follow the process, you will begin living your dream faster than seems possible by committing only five minutes a day.

STAY ON TRACK THE FIRST 30 DAYS

The first 30-days of your *Achieve in 5!* program are the most important if you are engaged in a long-term goal or an ongoing accomplishment. The first 30-days will set you on the path to creating *Achieve in 5!* as a practice.

If your goal is a one-time event, for example you want to clean your closet or organize the pantry. Then creating *Achieve in 5!* as a practice is not as important. The first 30 days are not as critical. However, if you have a longer-term project that you have put off and you want to complete, follow this thirty day prescription. If you use *Achieve in 5!* as prescribed during these first 30 days, you will see the power it possesses.

Think of the first thirty days as making one full lap around a running track. Keep this image in mind and stay right on the track. Each day gets you that much closer to a full lap.

Follow the guidelines previously presented for days 1–7. Then follow the guidelines below for days 8–30.

YOUR FIRST PROJECT

If this is your first time using *Achieve in 5!*, pick a project that you believe will take at least 30 days to complete by doing it five minutes each day.

START SLOW

When I start a new exercise routine, it feels so good to get back in shape that I go full speed and often work out at the gym two to three hours at a time. I love the feeling of getting in shape, but then I miss a day. Then I miss two days. Then I miss a week, and I am back to the old habits.

Achieve in 5! is exactly the same. If you start slow you can sometimes spend more time, but you must always remember that five minutes is your only commitment. You are more likely to succeed by starting slow. If you go full blazes the fire is likely to get extinguished quickly.

ONCE DAILY

Achieve in 5! means that you commit to five consecutive minutes once a day. Five one-minute actions will not have the same impact as one five-minute action.

It is also counterproductive to try to do two or three five-minute actions in one day. This is a huge set-up for failure. Stick with one *Achieve in 5!* project and work on it for five consecutive minutes, once a day.

AT BEDTIME

Each night, while lying in bed, right before you doze off, visualize your finish line and your dream on the other side of that finish line. Enjoy the feeling of success.

UNDER 30

During the first 30 days, it is important that you try not to work more than 30 minutes a day on your *Achieve in 5!* project. Remember, you are only committing to work five minutes a day. You do not need to work more than five minutes a day. Five minutes is success. If you are on a roll and go more than five minutes, that's good too, but please do not put the pressure on yourself ever to go more than five minutes a day.

It is extremely important that you establish a mindset that five minutes is okay. Therefore, you do not want to go more than 30 minutes or you will begin to put pressure on yourself to do more than five.

PLAN FOR SUCCESS

If your *Achieve in 5!* activity is to write a book, know that you will need your computer and possibly some research materials. Have everything at hand when you begin. *Achieve in 5!* starts when you start writing. It doesn't start when you start looking for your computer or looking for the notes you took while you were standing in line at the grocery store.

If you are cleaning your closet, *Achieve in 5!* means the time you are actually moving things out of your closet or putting them in your closet. The time you are going to the store to pick up all of those things you need to organize is preparation time, not *Achieve in 5!* time. So take the time you need to prepare to *Achieve in 5!* Then spend the *Achieve in 5!* time actually doing the work.

CELEBRATE

At the end of each week, take a minute or two to celebrate, giving yourself positive reinforcement. Place a gold star on the calendar, buy yourself some flowers, do something to show you have succeeded and feel good about your progress.

THE MORE YOU PRAISE AND CELEBRATE
YOUR LIFE, THE MORE THERE IS IN LIFE
TO CELEBRATE.—OPRAH WINFREY

THE *ACHIEVE IN 5!* CHALLENGE

*I*f you have a quick project or if you are not ready to commit to *Achieve in 5!* as a lifelong practice, try the *Achieve in 5!* Challenge. It is five minutes a day, five days a week, for five weeks.

Are you ready to start the challenge?

First, select your area of focus. Make it narrow and simple, but something where you will see results. You could:

- Clean a closet, a drawer, or a room.
- Start a simple exercise program.
- Write a magazine article.
- Begin writing in a journal.
- Meditate.
- Draw.
- Begin to play a musical instrument.
- Practice a foreign language.
- Begin a job search.
- Start a blog.

- Begin spending quality time with your partner or child.
- Enhance your knowledge in one area by reading five minutes a day.

Now that you have your topic, find a friend who will support you in your *Achieve in 5!* Challenge. Someone who will do it with you is best. That person does not have to take up the same topic. He should take the Challenge with his own interest.

Once you have completed the *Achieve in 5!* Challenge, you may be ready to take on a longer-term project.

CONTINUING THE JOURNEY

*A*lthough spending five minutes a day every day on your project may seem completely doable at this moment—and it is—from my experience it is a challenge for some people. In fact, I find it is a challenge for many people at some time. Keep in mind, *Achieve in 5!* itself is a discipline. I liken it to meditation, exercise, or following a healthy diet. It is a practice that takes time and commitment. It doesn't happen automatically. There is nothing that the process can do to make you follow it consistently. You have to do that. It is like brushing and flossing your teeth. You cannot miss a day or two and then make it up the following day by brushing and flossing longer or more times that day. The only way to truly benefit is to follow a daily routine.

If you miss a day, the next day just pick up where you left off. Do not think of *Achieve in*

5! as something that you HAVE to do. Remember, one of the achievement principles is, "I can quit." There is no falling behind or catching up with *Achieve in 5!*. It is like other disciplines. If you make it a practice to meditate 20 minutes a day and you miss one day, on the next day you would not say, "Oh no, now I have to meditate 40 minutes today." Even if you might try to double up the next day, I am almost certain that if you missed six days you wouldn't say, "Oh that's okay, I'll just meditate two hours today and I'll be back on track." If you are thinking this way about *Achieve in 5!*, you are missing the point and robbing yourself of the power of the discipline.

Once practiced consistently for months, *Achieve in 5!* will become like brushing your teeth. If you forget to brush your teeth one morning or if you were traveling and didn't have access to a toothbrush, you certainly wouldn't say, "Oh no, I didn't brush my teeth today. I failed. This is too hard to do every day. This brushing your teeth thing doesn't work."

If you miss a day, it is not the end of the world, it does not mean you failed, it does not mean you have fallen behind, it just means you need to get back in the routine and start again as soon as you possibly can. Do not let a missed day derail your dream. Your dreams depend on this journey.

Having a support group is one way to keep you on track. Know that you *can* achieve your dreams by committing five minutes a day. And know that you *will* succeed if you stay on track and continue the discipline.

You can and will, *Achieve in 5!.*

GO CONFIDENTLY IN THE DIRECTION OF
YOUR DREAMS. LIVE THE LIFE YOU HAVE
IMAGINED.   – HENRY DAVID THOREAU

BONUS SECTION

- Frequently Asked Questions
- 50 things you can achieve in five minutes a day
- Resources

BY FAILING TO PREPARE, YOU ARE
PREPARING TO FAIL.—BEN FRANKLIN

FREQUENTLY ASKED QUESTIONS

Q. How long will it take for me to see results with *Achieve in 5!*?

A. It depends on your project. Some projects can be completed in five minutes while others may take a few years. *Achieve in 5!* is a long term solution to an often longtime struggle. That said, regardless of how big your goal, if you work five minutes a day, every day on your goal, you should begin seeing progress within two weeks.

Q. Can I do more than one project at a time?

A. Remember the Chinese proverb, "The man who chases two rabbits catches none.?" I know *Achieve in 5!* sounds so easy that it seems like you could do two or three at a time. I have seen time and time again when a person tries to do two or three *Achieve in 5!* actions and ends up doing none. It becomes overwhelming and the individual loses the ability to focus.

Q. My project is huge and will take years to complete if I only work on it five minutes a day.

A. If you are not working on your project at all right now, years from now you will have made no progress. Start with five minutes a day, every day and see where you are in a month.

Q. Are there some projects that won't work?

A. I guess it depends on what you mean by "won't work." You can do aspects of almost any project with *Achieve in 5!*. But of course there are things that don't easily lend themselves to *Achieve in 5!*. Running a marathon is an example.

Q. I still don't understand why I can't work ten minutes one day if I miss my five minutes the previous day.

A. Think of it like brushing your teeth. If you forget to brush your teeth one day, you might brush longer and harder the next day, but that really doesn't make up for not brushing your teeth every day. You do not want to get into the habit of saying, "Well I'll do twice as much tomorrow." That is a recipe for quitting.

Q. What is the biggest thing that has been achieved using *Achieve in 5!*?

A. I don't know the biggest thing achieved, but this book was written using *Achieve in 5!*.

Q. I don't think five minutes can help. How can this possibly work?

A. Take the *Achieve in 5!* Challenge and see for yourself. See pages 121-122.

Q. You say stick to only one *Achieve in 5!* project. Why can't I do two or three *Achieve in 5!* projects at the same time, it's only ten minutes.

A. Over time, most people who stick with *Achieve in 5!* as a practice realize that one project is all they can really handle. You can always do more, but to identify more than one *Achieve in 5!* project creates competing priorities.

Q. How will exercising five minutes a day help me make progress toward losing weight and a flat stomach?

A. There are several resources for exercising five minutes a day that can help you get in shape. You can find them at www.achievein5.com and http://pinterist.com/achievein5.

Q. **Where can I find an** *Achieve in 5!* **support group?**

A. You could get a few friends or colleagues together to create a support group, or if you cannot find someone send an email to info@achievein5.com and we will try to put you in touch with a support group or an *Achieve in 5!* coach. Also join us on http://Facebook.com/achievein5

Q. **My biggest struggle is losing weight. How can I use** *Achieve in 5!* **to lose weight?**

A. Losing weight is usually a lifestyle change. *Achieve in 5!* can be helpful with lifestyle changes. You can take actions toward that lifestyle change by selecting successive *Achieve in 5!* milestones. You might start by simply spending five minutes a day documenting your feelings and what you ate that day. Once you understand your eating habits and triggers, you can spend five minutes a day creating a meal plan. You could also start with a five minute a day exercise plan.

Q. **What are some of the biggest challenges to** *Achieve in 5!*?

A. There seem to be two major challenges for people. The first challenge is clearly identifying their milestones. The first milestone should take you out of your comfort zone. This is hard for people to do. The second challenge, believe it or not, is sticking to five minutes a day. Having a support system helps with this one. For help with either of these challenges, refer to the *Resource Guide* in this section of the book.

Q. **How will I know when I have reached each milestone?**

A. Before you start your *Achieve in 5!* actions toward a milestone, you need to clearly define the milestone. You must have the milestone so clearly defined that you will know without question when it is reached.

Q. **If my** *Achieve in 5!* **goal is to change a habit, how will I know that the habit is changed?**

A. In setting your concrete milestone, you will want to answer that question for yourself.

Q. I don't think I have even five minutes a day to devote to this.

A. We all have many things to balance in life. If you have something you truly want to accomplish because it is your dream, you will be able to find five minutes a day to move it forward.

Q. I am over fifty years old. I don't have years and years to work on fulfilling my dream five minutes at a time.

A. Remember *Achieve in 5!* is a practice. After the initial period, you can work more than five minutes a day on your goals. The key is that you only commit to five minutes a day and that you work at least five minutes a day. By following this practice, you will find that you are moving toward living your dream faster than you had ever imagined. As author C. S. Lewis said, "You are never too old to set another goal or to dream a new dream."

50 THINGS YOU CAN *ACHIEVE IN 5!*

1. Clean a closet
2. Market a product
3. Start a fitness routine
4. Cook healthy meals
5. Start a meditation practice
6. Develop your social network
7. Keep in touch with friends
8. Become a better manager
9. Organize your office
10. Declutter your home
11. Learn to dance
12. Learn a foreign language
13. Teach your dog new tricks
14. Research your genealogy
15. Get your finances in order
16. Do an art project
17. Learn to play a musical instrument
18. Paint a room
19. Plant a garden
20. Find a new job
21. Start a business
22. Build a business
23. Change a habit
24. Expand your comfort zone

25. Reduce stress with five-minute relaxation techniques
26. Build a website
27. Read a book
28. Increase your knowledge of current events
29. Improve your relationships
30. Make a quilt
31. Play with your children
32. Make pillow covers
33. Relax with short films
34. Begin healthy living
35. Get published in a magazine
36. Learn a software program
37. Learn any new skill
38. Write in your journal
39. Begin to scrapbook or another craft
40. Volunteer with a nonprofit
41. Practice yoga
42. Commit random acts of kindness
43. Make jewelry
44. Meet someone new
45. Take a course (there are five minute courses)
46. Improve your vocabulary
47. Improve your memory
48. Improve your reading skills
49. Improve your self-image
50. Write a book

RESOURCE GUIDE

There are many resources available to help you succeed and *Achieve in 5!*; and the resource list is growing.

The blog provides general information about *Achieve in 5!*, tips for success and other resources:
www.achievein5.com

Up to the minute information, tips and ideas can be found by joining us on twitter:
www.twitter.com/achievein5

Join us on Facebook at:
www.Facebook.com/achievein5

For links to articles related to *Achieve in 5!* projects go to: www.pinterist.com/achievein5

And, feel free to contact me at:
Lesa@Achievein5.com

FAITH IS TAKING THE FIRST STEP EVEN
WHEN YOU DO NOT SEE THE
WHOLE STAIRCASE.—MARTIN LUTHER
KING, JR.

ACKNOWLEDGEMENTS

The content of this book was created when working with my clients and talking with friends about the way *Achieve in 5!* worked and discussing what didn't work for some people. Special thanks go to Aaron Estis an "old" high school friend who reappeared in my life, thanks to Facebook, just in time to edit the first version of this book. I give great appreciation to my God-daughter Aubrie Johnson, who is a young talented writer, and also provided much editing support. I am grateful to my friend, Luis Brown who was my most challenging participant, questioning every aspect of the process, which of course only made it better. I am deeply appreciative of Karla Robinson who did an amazing editing job on the first draft, resulting in significant revisions. I thank Judy Reesha who was a phenomenal editor of the final drafts. I cannot imagine the book being published without her eagle eye. I also thank my many Facebook friends and those that "Liked" the original *Achieve in 5!* on Facebook and took the 30 day challenge. I send a big thank you to Jennifer Pitcher for her support and for introducing Zita Pitcher to *Achieve in 5!* and to me. Zita was the most positive supporter of *Achieve in 5!* during the thirty day Facebook event a few years ago. I thank all who participated in the Facebook event and shared their experience participating in the program. A special thanks to my niece, Rien Sichini, who read the book and asked questions to ensure clarity. A sincere and heartfelt thank you to my sister, Fay Guilian, who has been supportive throughout the years. She is always there to help me think through a challenge. Sisters are truly forever. Finally, a giant thank you to my husband, Robert Hammond, who encourages, supports and provides the most positively constructive feedback of anyone I know. I also thank all of my friends and participants who have used *Achieve in 5!* and some who unknowingly offered stories for this book.

THE AUTHOR

 Lesa Hammond is the founder and president of Achievement U, Inc. a nonprofit organization created to inspire and empower young people by exposing them to relatable role models and new experiences. Known for her ability to coach individuals in career transition, Lesa has provided career and human resources advice to broad audiences. She has appeared as a guest on radio talk shows and been interviewed for several magazine articles. Formerly the expert from the Internet column *Ask Dr. Lesa*, she now focuses on helping people achieve their dreams and overcome scarcity thinking.

Lesa is the author of *Achieve in 5!*, *The Achievement System*, and the *Thompson Twins* book series—a middle-grade reader introducing children to Everyday Role Models by inserting

141

real people into fictional adventures. Her interests, research and passion center around transformative learning and act as a catalyst to help others overcome scarcity consciousness so that they may learn to dream and achieve their dreams.

Lesa holds a Bachelor of Arts in Sociology and Criminal Justice, a Masters of Public Administration with an emphasis in Human Resources, and a PhD in Transformative Studies.

NEVER GIVE UP ON WHAT YOU REALLY
WANT TO DO. THE PERSON WITH BIG
DREAMS IS MORE POWERFUL THAN THE
PERSON WITH ALL THE THOUGHTS.
ALBERT EINSTEIN

Please keep in touch:
lesa@achievein5.com
Join @Achievein5 on twitter
Blog: www.achievein5.com

If you are a life coach, therapist, or educator and
are using *Achieve in 5!* in your practice, I'd love
to hear how you are using it.
Email me: lesa@achievein5.com

Made in the USA
Charleston, SC
03 September 2013